More to Talk About

when seeking answers... not solutions

AF665025

Pravin Rai

BookLeaf Publishing
India | USA | UK

Made with ❤ on the BookLeaf Publishing Platform
www.bookleafpub.in
www.bookleafpub.com

Acknowledgments

As we go through this collection of poems, we'll be quick to realize that the writings are on purpose... or rather, the lack of it—perhaps about its absence. The universe, this nature & its creations; or people, ourselves—and our inventions like artificial intelligence—each at their own degree of purposelessness.

To that, I would argue the book is a few steps behind... or ahead! Depending upon perspectives. It is more about seeking—and that finding purpose is one of the many sought.

There are several dimensions to this collection & its eventual publishing; each layered, at different points in time. Broadly, it's either about emptying overflowing chatter containers within or filling up certain voids with intent. Although each has distinct motivations, there is a merging & blurring of boundaries. Distilled from these is the essence—a purpose. The words! These poems! This collection!

I acknowledge & thank my near and dear ones for giving me the experiences, encouragement & spaces to seek beyond the superficial. To think of purpose. The tangible outcome of which is this initial collection of poems.

The process started with a surprise few words as lines that popped from somewhere, which I then chose to expand on. And somehow found rhyming words—or not—that could flow in the rhythm of a poem. And more than the outcome, I found the process very fulfilling.

Of those that I have written, the ones probably relatable, thus shareable, are in this collection. There are many that are not... yet dear to me for having captured the essence of that particular moment.

While I mentioned above that words pop out, they are in reality triggered by occurrence—in real life or in thought. I would like to acknowledge the situations—and people therein—that lead to the process of getting these words out as poems to share.

People—rather, their invisibility—become quite obvious in these poems. These are about feelings abstracted from day-to-day interactions & anonymized to keep them personal yet public. Not by default that happens to be so... but by design to keep it so.

Keeping the spirit of chosen anonymity—also known as privacy—I acknowledge their contribution. And I am thankful for their presence in their respective dimensions within the layers of the collection.

Preface

Setting expectations would perhaps be prudent for this disparate, diverse, and disconnected collection of informal poetry. Each poem stands on its own; a few have been bunched as a theme.

More to Talk About is a book—much like conversations with ourselves—not expected to be read in sequence or cover to cover. Shifting topics, jumping back & forth, repeating a few, skipping some, even sharing with another a chosen few.

For the first read, it is suggested to have a quick glance through and get an essence of the collection as such.

Thereafter, return to those poems or sections that did resonate. Get a deeper understanding of the writer's intentions with the words chosen. In subsequent perusal—after this insight—an alternate perspective may emerge, reflecting broader dimensions

Operating instructions: Begin with no expectations. Judge for yourself, but only after a second read.

Share!

Contents

i got God, with words!

—

__i got God, with words!__ contrasts between expectation & experience. Many times we do not get what was asked for, yet disproportionately more of something similar—leaving a void for the desired—yet having got more... & that's confusing!

—

i got a poem
All i need is to find
the right words

i got flowers
All i needed was
a hug

i got a fortune
All i needed was
enough to give back

i got an education
All i need now is
common sense

i got well-wishers
All i need is
a friend

i got respect
All i needed was
love

i got a house
All i needed was
a place called home

i got an insurance
All i needed was
a sense of security

i got belief
All i needed were
values to go by

i got religion
All i needed was
Satsang, to seek

i got God
All i needed was
Someone to watch over me

Miracles
We all wish for
Hope is all we need!

Pay it Forward

—

***Pay it Forward** is a commentary on not having the ability or capacity to return favors to our Givers—our heritage, nature, parents, ancestors & humanity as a whole.*

The poem elaborates on the ancient wisdom of connecting our acts of prayer, charity, conservation, practice (study), and gratitude to the paths to repay our debts.

In concept & culture, these are integral to many of our practices. The underlying principle being paying forward for the sustenance of future generations.

—

Blessings, pay back
Blessed we are
For we arrived
As we are
In this world

Blessings are debts upon us
We can never refuse or return

Only pass forward, On our turn
The debt,
The blessings

Pay back Blessings

The reality is you can never pay back for what
you have got @birth!
One can only strive to leave behind a better
place than when you arrived

Nature

Our space for existence

which is everything around us
The environment, Earth
The entire universe.

pay back through
Prayers

Heritage
our history, evolution
learnings & culture

pay back through
studying & practicing

Ancestors
our lineage, family tree, their genes,
their ability to survive, so that we could be

pay back through
Gratitude

Living Beings
plants & animals, flora & fauna
Us, all that live & die.

pay back through
Conservation

Humanity
A gift only to our kind
Awareness,
consciousness, empathy

pay back through
Charity

Strive to leave a
better place than when you arrived
Perhaps the only way to pay back
&
Stay Blessed

Why we Lost our Tails

—

Why we Lost our Tails *is a non-scientific commentary on the evolution of mankind into a clever species; why abandoning the tail was necessary in favor of deception.*

—

The tail,
an extension
of the spine

Instinctive & reflexive
displays true state
of heart & mind

Tailless—now a lesser Spine
expressions cannot escape
captive in the mind

We lost our tails
So we could hide our feelings.
talk but not reveal the inside

For any insidious play
A wagging tail
a sure giveaway

Will not deceive
would not fall in line
cannot get enslaved by the mind

Of little use to Mankind

wobbly tail out of the way
none to tell tales on the mind

We lost our tails
So we would stand straight.
And walk in a stride

We lost our tails
It went out of evolutionary fashion.
No longer a display of pride

When we lost the Dictionary But could not stop talking

—

When we lost the Dictionary But could not stop talking *ponders on our unique ability to communicate in words.*

What would it be like if words lose their meanings? Did the birds ever talk?

—

Nothing made sense
Words with no meanings
Alphabets jumbled up

Yet we spoke
We met, we played
Smiled & laughed

Thoughts were clear
Relations intact
Life went on

When we did cry
No more "tell me why"
No further did those sorrows multiply

Bad words, fancy ones
Prose, poetry, or Prayers
All the same

interpret for yourself
Those feelings behind
As suits your mind

When we lost the Dictionary

Words no longer free
Show your deeds,
deliver by action

Words but, cannot entrap
Spirits flying high
Just hear those birds in the sky

Gestures, expressions
body language, for all to see
No whispers. No confessions

Between friends,
a glance
to say it all

When we lost the Dictionary

debates within, intense
words, no meanings, no end
Neither me, nor I, do bend

Quiet, deep inside,
A Thesaurus of Expressions
We discover ourselves

Awaiting words
to stop talking

Postscript

Birds and butterflies,
grammar of their own

Elephants and ants,
rulebooks with no words

Did they lose their Dictionary!
Did someone steal their Words...

Pangaea

—

Pangaea—the supercontinent—in a series breaking apart gave us the continents. Initially two—one for each hemisphere—and subsequently in the numbers we have today.

—

Nothing is forever.
Not even the land,
on which we stand.

"All the Land"

Long, long time ago.
A quarter billion years, or so.

Pangaea A vast supercontinent,
Held "all the land" on the planet.

One humongous landmass, alone & sole,
Centered at the equator, spanning
pole-to-pole.

Not paradise—no Adam nor Eve; none of our
ancestors around.
Primates took 200 million years more to walk
this ground.

Marine life in abundance; on land crawled
roaches & reptiles.
Those were the creatures of the times.

"Great Dying"

Something triggered mass extinction—an
ecological void.
Had a comet struck Earth? Or was it a giant
asteroid?

Perhaps many volcanic eruptions, bubbling
with inner rage?
Turbulent were the times; it was a desolate
age.

The "Great Dying," so harsh and violent.
Lost were forever, most species—over 90
percent.

"Miracles & Mutations"

Earth—eternal, so special—was destined for another fate.
Life that had survived, began to rejuvenate.

Miracles & mutations. Evolution at play.
Old made way for the new; that is nature's way.

Repopulated the planet, species anew—plants & animals.
Appeared, the early dinosaurs & first tiny mammals.

"Land Broke Apart"

Tremendous were the changes.
Few sudden, some slow, others in stages.

Environmental forces pushed waters toward land.
Sea in the east (Tethys), breached the equatorial band.

Mantle floated, land rifted, Pangaea broke apart.
Two continents set off to a fresh start.

Laurasia to the north.
Gondwana to the south.

Note

Movements in the mantle (due to convection currents that roll over in the mantle's upper zone) cause the plates to move slowly across the surface of the Earth.

Over time, Laurasia further broke apart, which became North America and Eurasia

Gondwana broke up to form the remaining continents.

In the *meantime Earth had witnessed several Mass Extinctions (ME) - Ordovician ME, Devonian ME, Permian ME (the Great Dying - 252 million years ago —the worst extinction event), Triassic-Jurassic ME (65 million years ago - ended the era of dinosaurs) & the Cretaceous-Tertiary (the K-T) ME . It is suspected that Earth is living through the 6th major ME.*

And... land kissed the sky

—

***Pangaea & And... Land Kissed the Sky...** are two poems, two hundred million years apart!*

A fraction of the 13 billion years of the existence of our universe, at the beginning of time.

As a part of this transition, until a hundred million years ago, the now-known Indian subcontinent was placed in the southern hemisphere. Eventually drifting northward.

And great landmasses met to birth the youngest, the tallest of mountain ranges—our Great Himalayas.

—

A,
long, long time ago.
100 million years,
or so.

A,
tectonic plate,
broke off to relocate.

Off,
on a voyage,
across hemispheres,
it sets forth.

Crossing,
the Tethys sea,
to the north.

For,
a 100 million years adrift.
and 150 million inches shift.

Moving,
inch-by-inch, year-after-year,
to a destination,
not so near.

In a tectonic odyssey,
Indian plate meets EurAsian.
thus begins a new quest.

As,
lands come together,
crashing & crushing,
in zest.

continental edges collide,
with energy unbound.

neither disengage,
nor cede ground.

pushing & jostling,
in a tectonic tussle.
both a match,
muscle-for-muscle.

Earth's crust crumples,
edges give way.

reshaping topology,
as time ticks away.

terrains elevate, peaks emerge,
...so high!

and...
land kisses the sky

the youngest.
the tallest.
the grandest.
to take birth

Heaven,
on our planet,
arises from Earth!

the
Himalayas

World War Tree

—

***World War Tree** is on a much much tinier time scale—but of potentially equally gigantic consequences.*

It tackles three aspects of the turmoil we are witnessing globally. The fact that it is our children losing lives for lands they will never again set foot on. The reality of claims & counterclaims on land, but not accounting for the people on that land. And finally, what is the way out?

—

At War?

Claim Victory
With trees

Not with flowers...
For your child!

World War Tree

All vanquished
But me, mine, ours
Country, Farms & Lands

Will it end
At that

After all that is what
wars are all about
Not the people

Land, or claims on it
Claim it if you can
With trees

Not with flowers...
For your child!

No choice
But WW Tree

Lend a tree your voice
Let forests voice claims
on their Land

With All Those Dreams We Go Away

—

With All Those Dreams We Go Away. *It is the material & the memories that we leave behind.*

—

Dreams!

The only thing we take away
All else stays back anyway

Memories, accumulate too heavy, left back
Dreams much lighter, an easy stack

Dreams true, untrue & forgone
A live maze connects life & beyond

A few come true, a few astray
Some precious, yet fade away

As life unfolds, dreams unpack
Merge, mix, emerge as a new rack

And when a Puzzled Soul loses its way
With All Those Dreams We Go Away

All else stays

Tricks of Time

—

Tricks of Time is about how time reveals its presence in our perceived world. Almost magical...

—

Birthed in the Cosmos,
measured by sunshine

intersects static space
Adds dynamism & pace

Interacts every Instant
each a new moment

Some call this time;
how else to define?

Makes its presence felt
A bundle of tricks

Is invisible. Is passing. Is endless
can't feel, see, hear, taste, or touch

Yet we miss, look forward & setup
Many a trick of time

Destiny of time, unclear
Goes one way, never the rear

Distance fixed,
whether far or near

Life, after-life, or no-life;
not it's affair.

Time changes
With No care

Punctual at all times;
an occasional " big bang " is fair

This life we live
Is it also a Trick

Alive till aware
Of moments marked

Some call it a lifetime
How else to define?

Yehi Hai
The Right Choice

—

Yehi Hai The Right Choice *is double-checking rational choices with inner instincts.*

—

Flip coins
Toss the die
Pick a card

How do you know
You made the right choice

Is there any way to check?
with your heart

Listen to the mind
Look for pros & cons
Make a SWOT chart
Collect data
Analyze
Decide

At the end
Flip the coin, toss the die
Take your pick of the card

Match the outcome of the toss
Feel that instant within

Elation or Loss?

That's the right choice
Heart did decide!

Cautionary Note
Pick up the coin, those dice
Or a pack of cards
At your own
Cost, Risk & Care
I ain't responsible!

Inner Truth

—

Inner Truth is a meditative piece across dimensions of awareness of the Self, detaching from external labels.

—

Naked Thoughts.
Naked is being undressed.
to the extent of feeling embarrassed.

Thoughts are being aware,
to an extent of feeling the emotions.

Aware of my nakedness!
Feeling embarrassed. —Within!

Naked Truth.
Naked is being undressed,
to the extent of feeling embarrassed.

Truth is being transparent,
Verifiable beyond doubt.

Naked is transparent.
Transparency brings truth. —Outside!

True Thoughts.

Truth is being transparent,
Verifiable beyond doubt.

Thoughts are being aware,
to an extent of feeling the emotions.

Thoughts... unverifiable, outside!
Emotions... truthful, within!

As we un-layer, un-dress, un-burden
Ourselves!

Ignoring thoughts.
Devoid of emotions.
Meet our inner truth.

Blissful.
in meditation.
Aware.
Me.
I

Ourselves!
AUM
(silence)

Seeking

—

Seeking *is a simple question each one of us has asked ourselves, at some point or another about existence & purpose. And gave up on getting a convincing response. This remains inconclusive... as always!*

—

who am i
beyond the obvious
behind unknowns
questions ahead unfold
past untold
who will you find
amongst those answers

am i
the opportunities missed
the cures not found
secrets that remain
for all times
even by God unseen
nor the devil ever met

seeking unknowns
that define

who i am

Greedful & Grateful

—

***Greedful & Grateful** highlights the place & value of time, over, and on top of abstract experiences Although we want our highs—and the lows that tag along—pacing it with love & life is just as critical. Too fast, too quick... may not be always desired.*

—

Time for the Greedful

What if, we could

Love,
And Live

All
Our future
Experiences

In one day
In an instant

Without compromise
No loss of Experiences
Joy
Sorrow, et al.

Would we
not take it?

Are we not
Greedy enough?
Would you take it?

Do not
you have
Greed

For more
Time?

Grateful for Time

Why Waste
What we
Already have got
And Like

Live!
Love every
Moment
Of it!!

Sad Days

—

__Sad Days__ is about our coping mechanism for dealing with the lows. There is a thin line between sad & not so.

—

Of the days i remember
Sad days are the most

Is it that i had a few
And that, those i cannot forget

Of the days i remember
Sad days are the least

Is it that i had a few
Yet, that i chose, to forget

Of the days i remember
Sad days are all i get

That i regret

Of the days i remember
Sad days do not exist

Did i forget the days
or the difference?

A Taste of Life

—

A Taste of Life explains how the best of plans could go sour on execution and how spontaneous instinctive actions remedy the worst.

—

Perfect Recipes

A perfect recipe
Exotic ingredients

Measured proportions
Precision cooking time

Visual appeal

A promise
A tasty delight

Bland
Once served

Pickling

An experience
Passed forward
By association

And shared secrets

An oily stench
Magical masalas
Each one of its own

Similar but unique

Raw Choppings
Many things, anything's
As & when they arrive

Adding & tasting
And then some more

A pickle jar
Oddly shaped
Stains of time

In shades & sunshine

No promises
Of consistency
Of optics
Of perfection

Once served
turns a bland serving
Spicy

Bland & Spicy

Such is life
No perfect recipes assure
Pickled uncertainties ensure
A Taste of Life

Chasing my Footprint

—

Chasing my Footprint *narrates the visuals of a casual evening stroll, with an underlying theme (if one chooses to draw that parallel) of our routines of daily life—some with purpose, many without.*

—

Evening strolls, around and about.
Breathe easy, or sweat it out.

Stylish lamp posts, background aglow.
Watchful eyes, glance for a hello.

Gentle breeze, lined up trees.
Familiar faces, with dogs on leash.

Many walk briskly, on concrete ground.
800 steps complete a round.

Some to lose weight, some to gain strength.
Each to their targets, of time or distance.

Start wherever.
Stop whenever.

Walk, jog, or break into a sprint.
In circles I go, chasing my own footprint.

Marching forward, round after round.
Getting nowhere, nor destination bound.

Many miles walked, a few milestones crossed.
In this circle of life, why's one lost?

Boredom or Bliss

—

***Boredom or Bliss** is about wasting or engaging with time—rather life. The trick is in transcending from the former to the latter.*

—

Free
of the Self inside
detached, ignorant

You, your
Thoughts, Time & Tasks
Unfulfilled bags of freedom

A freely dangling
empty bag of Boredom
a wasted freedom

Free
of the worlds around
detached, explores

You, your
Thoughts, Time & Tasks
Bags filled with freedom

Happiness inside
A fulfilling freedom
Bliss

Boredom or Bliss
Extremes of freedom

Scaffolds have no Storey

—

Scaffolds have no Storey *describes how greatness is built by invisible support structures. A story on how storeys got built.*

—

Scaffolds
in empty skies

indeed were up before
helping hands at the fore

For man & material
to scale those highs

Scaffoldings held tight
Stood firm, at all & any height

/

Structures
emerge in wonder

which sky, what star
they'll be under

House's of Governance
or those for Justice

Monuments to tell us
History happened, not to repeat

Sacred spaces
when prayer & blessings meet

purposed structures
for caring, when unwell

homes away from home
for merchants & travelers

Pillars that bridge opposites
Shores that never meet

Floors in air, they borrow
a space for tomorrow

/

Structures built, got their story
debris gone, came the glory

Scaffolds dismantled, had no Storey
out of sight, out of memory

/

All have had scaffolds as we grew,
watching over us as we flew

we stand firm on ground
Our scaffolds moved around

Quietly framing, structuring
dreams in empty sky

Another storey
Another's story

Ourselves

—

***Ourselves** highlights the vulnerability of the perpetrators of misdeeds. And questions whether it touches their conscience… ever!*

—

Do thieves lock their homes,
as they go out for yet another heist
Knowing that there are others out there

Do hackers keep strong passwords
As they bank & share stories of their spoils
Knowing that there are others out there

Do molesters worry for their own
As they go out with familiar or unknown
Knowing that there are others out there

Do the corrupt feel any guilt
As they accuse & punish for lesser misdeeds
Knowing that there are others out there

Does anyone feel the disgust
As others shower insults to feel respected
Knowing that you are also out there

Pointless... for a Purpose

—

__Pointless... for a Purpose__ metaphorically maps the dependency of finding & fulfilling our purpose—our inner callings—on the outside world. It can never be a solo journey, with no reference or observer.

—

Every time, I pass by
that lane on my path

a dog caged barks

in disgust & anger
stuck in 4x4 compound

the dog knows & I know
both are bound

I cannot abandon my path
Nor he, his purpose

Pointless
I find the caged barking meaningless
As the dog sees me strolling that path

Pointless, a lifetime bound
In a confined mind, or compound

Despite, every time one passes by
Another finds a mission, to live by

Our paths taken
pointless... for a purpose

Secure in Hate;
Love Insecure

—

Secure in Hate, Love Insecure *touches upon the twisted psychology of hate and how it is winning against love in a polarized world.*

—

Hate!

Quick to find, Friends
And we love, These Hateful, Friends

We share, The same, Hate
A common, Hate

A meeting, Of minds
A sense of, Belonging

Secure, In Hate

Love!

Quick to seek, Commitment
And we hate, loveless Commitments

Do we share, The same, Love
A meeting, Of hearts?

Is there a common Bond?
Or a sense of, Bondage?

In Love, Insecure

Fate is in the Past

—

Fate is in the Past *provides a unique perspective on fate & destiny and why we cannot change destined outcomes—so easily.*

—

Fate. Destiny.
All are in past tense.
One knows only after the fact.

And we cannot change the past!
That's why we cannot change our
Fate. Destiny.

This is the Chakrayudh.
Of life.

Quick to get in.
Get out, cannot
Alive!

Reverse steps, if you can
Get to the beginning of the past.

There you go,
with one more chance to define
Fate. Destiny

With a Life purpose
This is Puna Janam,
re-born with a destination

Can we do it?
In one lifetime?

Aloof

—

__Aloof__ is "inspired" by families together under a common roof, living apart behind well-architected walls, marking out space for each. And how these have transformed into private territories of time & activity.

—

We live aloof,
Under one roof!

Behind the door,
There are four.

A common hall,
And room for all.

Smartphones in hand,
All streaming broadband,

Personal stories, none to share.
With Youtube, however, there's no care!

Blu-ray station & TV in high definition,
Laptop & speakers in wireless configuration.

Seldom meet friends.
WhatsApp messaging serves to this end.

Guests are rare,
Parties we do not dare!

We live aloof,
Under one roof!!

Limited face-time.
Unlimited screen-time.

There's Google for knowledge,
And Coursera for college.

With Amazon we shop, lazing in bed,
Check out Zomato, avoid cooking instead!

Staggered meal times,
Floating bed-times.

An occasional pleading.
The usual stonewalling.

Monologues of despair.
Dialogues, a yelling affair.

An uncertain future,
An indifferent past,

If coexistence is to stay...
Keeping distance seems to be the way.

We live aloof,
Under one roof!

Forgot How to Smile!

—

Forgot How to Smile! *is an abstraction of the inner loneliness from the apparent and visible bonhomie amongst social settings.*

—

Laughter now louder
Often I wonder

The jokes no funnier
Sense of humor, only worse

Funny bones calcified
Dopamine rush, I wish it was

Happiness index, can't say
Not much joy coming our way

Is laughter of the crowd
Trampling a solo smile?

Where are
those innocent smiles

Friendly nods, firm handshakes
Approving glances

Words in loving nuances
Gone are the subtle vibes

Forgot, how to smile
Now I only laugh

...at myself!

Fragile, is what

—

***Fragile, is what:** When there is no option to hide,*
only can run. If vulnerable… keep distance.
Distance is the only cover if exposed.

—

Fragile is what
I know now

No margin
for error

One misstep
Crumbling, all comes down

At the mercy of the other
Not to throw a stone

Fragile is what,
I know now

Fragile is that,
I know how

guards down
once trustingly close

rocks out
in open, strewn around

Fragile is that,
I know how

Keeping away
only way to stay

At the mercy of distance
Not at stone's throw away

Fragile is what
I know now

Dependable

—

***Dependable** is not indispensability. Nor does it make the other dependent. Likewise, independence is not separation.*

—

Dependable Independent
Sun & its Shine

Sun holds its Shine
Time taken for granted

Shine does escape
wakes up to sunshine

Why seek someone dependable
Not because you are dependent

Why seek independence
Not because you can

Is being independent
Same as being separate

Is being the indispensable
Same as being doomed, stuck

Some spend all of life
Seeking someone dependable

The others, spend it all
Seeking to be independent

Some see the other to be
as independent, as can be

Others see themselves to be
as dependable, as can be

Few know the difference

Take for granted
Dependence sets in

Escaping indispensability
Time in darkness

Wake up to Sunshine
Independent & dependable

Dependable Independent
Sun & its Shine

Every Breeze has a Soul

—

***Every Breeze has a Soul**: For most of our worries, a solution is already within us. It takes a gentle breeze—a metaphor for the soul—to trigger self-resolution.*

—

Every Breeze has a Soul
A living Soul
Like You, me, us

A touch of the breeze
Anger goes away, evaporates
Cools with your own sweat

A sensation of ever-present air
A smile comes your way, cheers
Reminds you, of your own joys

A ruffling of the hair
Lovingly perks the mood, energizes
Resonates within you, to make your day

Make your day & those around
For you to touch
Like the breeze

A living Soul
Like You, me, us

Postscript
The joy, the remedy, the peace
All the goodness
Is within

It some times,
Rather, most of the times
Needs the kindness of a breeze

To make your day
Your life!

We Got it All Wrong

–

***We Got it All Wrong** goes deeper in understanding of the metrics we apply in our daily narrations. Are we measuring the things we ought to?*

—

For greatness
We measure height
It should be depth

For bigness
We look at weight
It's vastness of the sky

For happiness
We seek absence of sorrow
Acceptance of truth it is

For trust
It is loyalty that matters
Reliable over time, it must be

For love
Intensity of time together is a measure
Should it not be emptiness while apart

For blessings
We attribute good luck over and above
Instead of steady balance at the core

For prayers
We picture never-changing infinites
It's the freshness of hope we breathe in

Did we get anything right
Not crying. Not laughing
For they could be misplaced

But a Smile on a Face
Can never go wrong

Always in its right place

Point of Views

—

***Point of Views** offers perspective in time & the optics therein. The question is, does the reality change as well for each fresh look?*

—

If we had eyes behind
Would that still be looking back

If we could look further ahead
Would that be called the future

If we could open eyes in sleep
Would dreams come true

If everything goes blurred
Would there still be dividing lines

With microscopic vision
Nothing too small to ignore

And with telescopic
No place too far to reach

Instead of two, if there were an infinite few
We'd be open to many a point of view

Eyes Cry Too

One downside with the eye
It also cries!.

With many
Would we know which one & why

Does reality really change with
another Point of View

We Need it All

—

We Need it All *talks of the different ways we engage with any incident. There's no right way or wrong. In times of crisis, we need it all.*

—

Sympathy

Every dark cloud
Has a shiny outline

Glow of kind hearts
Feeling heavier than the cloud

Consolation

Every misery
Has a story to be told

Flow of kind words
Hollow echos.

All directions

Charity

Every storm
Has a lull as it begins

Calm in the end
Cooling winds, felt again

Sympathy, Console, Charity
it's not either or

When storms happen
when things go wrong

We need it All

Poisoned Ambrosia

—

***Poisoned Ambrosia:** A wish coming true may not always be the thing, to have wished for as the past tags along.*

No matter how much of "good" one gets, there's no wishing away the past.

—

Outlive our real memories
That we already do

Dreams no more, of a future
Those of past fill in instead

That one about eternal life
Ambrosia promised so

An angel, a hero, —a name
A claim to fame

To be Remembered forever
That's a dream, that remains

Memories of that dream
My future of that time

That one about eternal life
Came with the "past" bundled along

Shaken awake in time
before was fully dreamt

Forever, is a long time
More than time can keep

An eternity of life past
Brought to present

Outlive our real memories
For a reason we always do

Poisoned Ambrosia

Opposite Directions

—

***Opposite Directions** is not being perfect, yet we dare. We resolve, negotiate, cooperate, and win facing each other not only in conflict but also as we move forward into an embrace.*

—

Away from perfect
We reached that goal

Aware of our faults
We healed ourselves

Allow for our needs
We felt one another

Able to stay ahead
We had someone behind

Aspire for true love
We sought not perfection

At last came in embrace
we moved, opposite directions

Away from perfect
We reached that goal

Don't Deny Your Child

—

***Don't Deny Your Child** is somewhat preachy, but can get us to start thinking about how times have changed and how not.*

—

Don't Deny Your Child
Her childhood
His freedom
Her curiosity

Her time to play
And learn
By themselves

His turn
To speak up
And be wrong

Her mistakes...
She would make
To learn

Give them all
What you were denied
Tech that didn't exist

Toys of today
Values of the day
Wisdom that stays
Give them love
And time
Let them know you're there

But not a bear hug
They also need space
To grow

Don't Deny Your Child
Yourselves
And themselves, as well

Dreams... too Big

—

Dreams... too Big *talks about mis-sized* dreams with no common theme. And not giving up despite.*

**mis-sized: overlapping & intersecting dreams, yet mismatch in dimensions... not exactly in size—big or small, near or far—but in scope, context, aspirations, settings, etc.*

—

I couldn't give up
On my dreams

How could I give up
On yours

With eyes shut
It didn't matter

I was only in mine
You in yours

Trouble came waking up
Focused, not given up

Narrow vision
Shrunk our worlds

Determined dreams,
no space for others

Dreams too big
...to watch Together

Couldn't fit
One screen

Postscript

Keeping our dreams together
set us all apart

We didn't deserve
Those nightmares

I Know, I Don't Know Paradox

—

I Know, I Don't Know Paradox *fits in well with the paradoxical flavors of many of the tales told through poems in this collection...*

—

I know, what I know
I don't know,
what I don't know

I know nations go to war
to "keep the peace"
I don't know who pays
"that price" for such peace

I know of "men"
losing lives over "no man's land"
I don't know if this ever solved
the disputes over land

I know polarization & pollution,
are "human creations"
I don't know which
will trigger "human extinction"

I know that positive outcomes
begin with right intentions
I don't know if one can preempt
"unintended" consequences

I know we get the leaders
we deserve
I don't know if the leaders
are deserving

I know that "knowledge"
is finite
I don't know the limits
of "ignorance"

I know not
to "talk with strangers"
I don't know how else
to make new friends
I know
"love is blind"
I don't know if I will
"see" love

I know the beginning
determines the “end”
I don’t know the end
that “precedes" the next beginning

I know “good deeds”
take one to Heaven
I don’t know if the scoring
is “relative” or “absolute”

I know, what I know
I don’t know,
what I don’t know

What do you know?
What don’t you?

Miracles, None Overnight

—

Miracles, None Overnight *talks of the real & relatable miracles in our daily lives—taken for granted.*

—

Miracles do happen
Sun shines our mornings bright
With a billion years of fire & light
A miracle, over the night, but is it overnight

Earth spins around all night
The miracle, that brings Sun to sight
Takes a miracle, to witness another

Cold, rainy, sunny, or night
Northern lights or tidal waves
Seasonal miracles in their own right

Seeds blown miles away, in windy flight
Blooming colors on hills bright
Miracle of flowers, always a delight

Our presence this day
sculpted from another
Miracles of a Mother

Miracles, a Creation
Tons of metal we propel into flight,
defying common sense & our fright
Miracle of science

When reality becomes virtual
And imagination comes to life
A miracle trick of the mind

That lonely voice, across the globe
A dozen digits, dial in whispers to your ear
Miracle bridge for hearts miles apart

Man on Moon & soon on Mars
And further ahead beyond the stars
Many more miracles to come

Dark matter, Black holes
Energy of the Soul
science may give up
miracles will not

Never ends.
Another Miracle!

Silence is Sound, not Reached...

—-

Silence is Sound, not Reached: *Who does that silence belong to? Is it yours to take or another to give? Silence from a new perspective.*

—-

Silence is Sound
not reached
yet! ...distant

Patience
with sound.
Quietens itself!

Listening
has its own
Dampening effect!

Echo Chambers
reflect within.
Listen... reflect some more!

Sound Embraces
dark shadows
that light left... behind!

Muddled Sound
filtered & timely unheard.
Cancels Noise!

Breach Barriers
get ahead of noise
Sonic Boom

Sound @Web-speed
Instantaneous
Netsonic*

*Note

Netsonic, a term coined to describe the speed of sound traveling on the internet; a term derived from supersonic, hypersonic. E.g., instant messaging platforms

A Missing Definition

—

***A Missing Definition** of life, of love. Both make their presence felt through feelings. And there is no one way to define either. An attempt has been made to set apart, a part of these feelings in opposite phases—of presence... and of absence.*

—

Absence you miss
Presence you miss
As well

Absence you are longing
Presence you are longing
For more

Absence you feel
Presence you feel
Even after

Absence is dreams
Presence is dreams
Coming true

Absence, all is lost
Presence, all is lost
to you.

Absence or Presence
Absence of vibes!
Presence of vibes!
apart in phase
Absence & Presence
A part of the phase

A missing definition

Some call
Love

Others
Life

Locked Locker Loot

—

***Locked Locker Loot** is about imagined losses & how they disturb us just as much as—perhaps more—if something tangible were lost.*

—

locked
was the locker, that was looted

unimaginable
was the pain, for the loss of an
imaginary gain

lost what? we wonder
by how much am I under?

was in there,
a written Will, which never will
or a treasure, with no measure

memories
a photo bundle, no more to fumble
a note of gratitude... or regret
that could not forget

a secret,
never to be told, written, for later to unfold
perhaps a key, with a number, for yet another
locked locker.

/

from the locked locker,
of that, that it did hold
the Will, the note, the bundle
or a secret not to be told

Invaluable to some,
for the looters, value was none

unmeasured treasure
perhaps had some gold.
but for the loot,
it would be forgotten, left unsold.

/

inside
the locked locker,
what was, remains untold

outside
grief for a speculative loss
did unfold

/

Locked lockers
do you have any yet
keys that you did forget

treasured memories
irreplaceable, invaluable
not mere objects

the vaulted nagging secret
a couplet or a note
you wrote,
but share
did not dare

secure what you value
unlock, unburden
before late,
leave not to fate

live, do not fret.
leave, with no regret!

///

The Law, The Land

in perspective of time

–

The Law, The Land*: It's high time we recognize time to be a critical feature not only for delivering justice but also for getting justice.*

—

Law & Justice... is fine
Is it in time?

Law of the land stands supreme
Nothing overshadows the law
Not even the truth
Not even time

/

Seeking, speaking & securing the truth
roles of law; perhaps it's goal
Truth is valid for a point in time
Lie is invalid for all time
Truth, could be a lie
once mismatched in time

/

Seeking justice
is seeking the truth,
of that point in time
Speaking justice
is also denying any lie
for that time

/

All things, in life,
have an expiry date
Value is zero, once in that state
It's justice
if redeemed & recovered; or a penance well
within the " best before " date
Beyond
It just is late
It's just it's fate

Calibration of Crime

Law measures crime
calibrated in units of time
denial of freewill
its delivery tool

Access to place & material
in dimensions of time

Justice delayed
is denying justice of time

Land remains unaffected
Law remains true to the land

Truth falls behind
in time

The law, The land

In the law of the land
justice of time
is an issue prime

Lack of Law for Time
Lack of Time in Law

Is it
Time for a Law for Time?

Power Games

—

***Power Games:** While the games people play on or above the surface are for all to see, the real power, in fact & in feature, is underground. Is the deep state.*

—

Tallest
Strongest

the Tower

Down below

Buried
Deepest

the Power

/

Battles in Between
Conquer the top

/

Host a Flag
Broadcast the arrival

Fluttering Power
Changes with the Wind

/

Power
Over people

For the land
Under

/

Gold, Oil, Minerals,
indeed Diamonds

Power
The Deep State

Faith in Fairness of Fate

—

Faith in Fairness of Fate: No one questions the side that shows up on a coin tossed despite the high stakes that could be tied to it. A sense of fairness in luck.

—

As a matter of faith
In the fairness of fate

The spinning side
Always on the edge
Just a matter of time

Fate Value

A smooth long spin ride
Or a wobbly start, quick to end
Falls flat on its face

Unseen, the losing side
Fate of that Time
Fate Value

Face Value

Flat down, not in motion
Symbols show up
the winner side

Symbols of fate
for all time
Face Value

Faith Value

Heads or Tails
Make or break

Outcomes
Beyond control

Yet accepted
As a fair choice
Not challenged
Nor debated

As a matter of faith
In the fairness of fate

Artificially Intelligent

—

***Artificially Intelligent** is a comment on lab-grown intelligence. Will emotions be synthetic as well?*

—

In-vitro Wisdom
Evolving in a petri-dish

Will Emotions be etched
in Silicon too?

Or Heartless with AI

AI vs. ai

—

AI vs. ai reiterates our fears of mankind being subjugated by Artificial Intelligence. Or will animal instincts prevail?

—

Will
tech over-create
even more than
The Creator

Can
innovation out-pace
Evolution

Does
cutting-edge blunt the
Primitive

Will
pursuit challenge
preservation

Can
processing power
contain
people power
to become,

the RISK!
Which
new frontier will test
our survival skills

Artificial Intelligence
Versus
animal instincts

What Prevails
Who wins Eventually...

Senseless Connections

—

***Senseless Connections** attempts to highlight the disconnect between the semantics, syntax & function by connecting the usage, logic & purpose of our senses in abstract scenarios.*
A piece on our senses & their disconnection with metaphorical usage.

—

In Blinding Lights.
We Drive!
Can't See the point.

Bottled Fragrances.
We Spray!
Wishing for a Scent of love.

Keeping Distance.
We Hug!
Missing the Human Touch.

Hungry for Attention.
We fight!
Leaves a bad Taste.

In Silence.
We Pray!
Does He Hear us?

Conscious Robots.
We Imagine!
Are we Aware of the hazards?

ESP & Clairvoyance.
We Wonder!
Is it for real or simply non-'Sense'?

Are we Being Discovered?

—

Are we Being Discovered? *is a seemingly improbable scenario where mankind & all its progression are pre-ordained in an Intelligence that is now discovering us as we follow the "path."*

"Stone age" to "Silicon age" are logically explainable, in hindsight. "Soul age" is TBD (to be discovered) by the discoverer… which may not be us!!

Are we the "discovered?"

—

Are we inventing
or is AI discovering us?

Sand to Soil
Sand to Silicon
Sand to Soul

/

Soulless, lifeless
Dead rock
10 billion years

Waiting
Awaiting the inevitable
Happening

Of life

Nurtured nature
For existence
And evolution

Transform
Rock to tools
And never stop

Until Tools evolved
With a Soul

Now they/we are there
Almost...

AI with A Soul
(R)evolution of the Tool

Happy... with what we don't have

—

Happy... with what we don't have: *Such will be the days in the coming era of abundance.*

—

What will bring happiness
To the soul?

Eternal happiness

Religion brought purpose
To the world

Farming brought certainty
To the wild

Education brought knowledge
To the masses

Philosophy brought reason
To the thinking mind

Sciences brought understanding
To those who asked

Industry brought opportunity
To those who could

Technology brought convenience
To civilization

Networks brought collaboration
To the isolated

Will
Artificial Intelligence bring an abundance of wealth?
Fission brings an abundance of power?
Space brings an abundance of lands?

Will that be the Ultimate Bliss?
Happy... with what we don't have

H!... Add a tinge of Evil

—

H!... Add a tinge of Evil: The next awakening of AI is imagined to be with human-like self-awareness & empathy for one another, thus the term Humane !ntelligent (exclamation is deliberate)... In this otherwise perfect world of AI, would we not be flawless like the Gods? Add a bit of "bad" in the algorithms to make it real!

—

Some time in the future.
An era beyond the current.

When AI is building itself
evolving, transcending...
The next big thing
Of that time.

H!
Humane !ntelligence
It is
(will be)

Omnipresent.
Omniscient.
Omnipotent...

Everywhere, all the time
Everything known, for all times
Everything possible, can do, anytime

Everything & even more!

Connects with all, in equal measure
Connects at all times, access is 24x7
Connects anywhere, without bias

Mistakes it makes, but seldom.
Mistakes to learn from, never repeat
Mistakes to teach a lesson, to itself.

Teaches all that is known & what will be too.
Teaches a lesson, before things go wrong
Teaches the rules, it made for you

Knows what ails you, decades ahead
Knows the cures & the consequences
Knows the prognosis prior to diagnosis

Secrets, keeps them all
Secrets each one's, in confidence
Secrets not yet known, at all

Keeps track of deeds, yet not done
Keeps scores, for the unruly game
Keeps in sync, within its universe

Powered by neurochips
Powered by waves that make dreams
Powered with human ingenuity
But
It will grow, bigger than we could fathom
It will learn, more than told & is known
It will have a mind of its own!

Creators' rules to rule

Every cheering is followed by some jeering
Every gift has a price to return
Every good deed at the cost of some bad.

Checked. Balanced.
With no friction, we wouldn't walk
With no resistance, society wouldn't evolve
With no evil, would we all not play God?

Add some bad to the calendar
Add some spice to life
Add a tinge of evil
You ain't God!

Future of Sins
...as we know it

—-

Future of Sins as we know it... *examines AI's impact on the Sins of Man, as defined in certain old literature. Is there a case of refining or redefining any of those?*

Perhaps add a few... for the machines!!

(References: Wikipedia: Seven deadly sins)

—-

When Intelligence
is designed,
Instincts, no longer desired

Measured, not the IQ
but chunks of data churns,
in neuro-unit scales

Capacity to regenerate
and to pioneer the next
Sourced out to giga-meta-machines

and these, available to all

/

Decisions, cannot go wrong
Investments, never go bad
Medicines, match each one's lifestyle

No sorrow, an algorithm cannot fix
Relations, always guided their best
Economy of abundant times

/

Sins, not easy to define

Pride... with no
power to decide
now kept aside

Greed... redefined
with so much to choose
and nothing to lose

Lust... no longer a thing to ignore
morality & physicality, not to interfere
Real if not, virtual always there

Envy... not of successes
"It's a machine thing"
Vanity, yet shall remain

Gluttony... won't matter
Satiated state of mind
with pulses, of the electric kind

Sloth... the way of life
Preferred over the creative type.
Master bots have insecurities too

Wrath still to fear
One-sided, though it'll be
when bots lose their mind!

/

Wonder
What would be the real sins
...Of artificial times?

On the path to Super Intelligence

—

***On the path to Super Intelligence**: History has shown that social & political structures create enemies to pick up a fight... for supremacy of the tribe & its leaders.*

Are we on the same path with Super Intelligence?

—

Quantum computing
Everything it'll know

But not the species
That it will control

Can it stop the wars
Can it feel for the dead

Can it choose from religion
The divine & not the divide

It will save lives for sure
From disease & hunger

Can it also undo that'll go
From greed & in anger

Winning at any cost
We willingly pay

We will teach the Ethics
Rules, those we can afford

Quantum computing
Everything you will know

But not
who will be in control

We create an enemy
To pick up a fight

That's why we will create
You!

Silence, you will never hear... again

—

***Silence, You Will Never Hear Again**, subtly describes the loudness of the unspoken—around & within. Quite like the poems in this collection—a lot is stated outside those lines—if one can hear that silence.*

—

How Far does Silence Go
Did it reach you... Ever

Have you spoken in Silence
And were heard

Did it mean the same
As was told

Was its language the same
Or lost in translation

your silence, did it begin with you...
and belong

Or borrowed
from the one's around

Does silence stop at you
As for another

Is it a cascade in forward flow
Determined, never to stop

Yet Fragile, easy to break
one odd thought: it does crack

How far does silence go
Blocked, would it echo back

Can you bear that silence
You never will hear

Again!

Lingering Fragrances

—

*Lingering Fragrances, **Too Close*** *is on feeling another's imprints & interaction of those vibes left behind, with a sense of familiarity.*

With fragrances as a metaphor, a narration of the lingering presences of one another in the same space & situation, long before.

A persisting feeling of one's presence.

—

Weren't we, too close
In each other's space
Traces of fragrance
Sensing presence

Weren't we, too aware
strangers together
Lingering fragrances
Greet the other

Weren't we, too silent
Listening each others'
Distinct fragrances
Diffused in air

Weren't we, too shy
Familiar Fragrances
Did the talking
For you, and i

Weren't we, too close
In each other's space
Lingering fragrances
Marked our times

We never met...
Yet presence felt!

Why do the deaf dance?

—

Why do the Deaf Dance? *touches upon how many of us lack the sensory capacity to perceive the good that comes into our lives; and wonder how & why others are so blissful.*

Inspired by
"And those who were seen dancing were thought to be insane by those who could not hear the music."
- Friedrich Nietzsche

—

Does she hear the melody?
Does she follow the beats?

Moving in rhythm, she syncs her pace
Does she feel the bass?

Can she hear the applause?
Or is there another cause?

Why do the deaf dance?

For euphonic notes, she may not hear
Harmonics do touch her soul so dear

Waves of sound may not reach
Her spirit makes the barriers breach

Playing within beats of her heart,
Passion for life, lyrics of love

Tuned to her inner music, she sways,
to the melody of the universe

Why do the deaf dance?
It's rather the inverse

Can you hear her music?
Do you hear her beats?

Can you follow the melody,
to which she taps her feet?

Earth & Ether...

—

Earth & Ether... is about how ancient wisdom had an all-encompassing explanation at a level much different than the theories of modern-day science. It provided context to the physical world, comprising of the basic five elements—Earth, Fire, Air, Water & Ether.

—

Earth & Ether...
and all else between!

Earth
however stable
Needs balance
To be sustainable
Before global warming
Brings a Catastrophe...

Air
however fresh
Needs exchange
To sustain life
Before inhale; Exhale
Breath control

Water
however holy
Needs to stream
To the lower plains
Before it floods over
Beyond course...

Fire
however sacred
Needs to extinguish
At some point!
Before it spreads
Beyond control...

Ether
however indistinguishable
Needs recognition
Explain the unknown
Before science discovers
Beyond Comprehension...

A Bookmark

—

***A Bookmark** is about friendships marking shifting moments.*

—

A reminder
Of the chapters
Unfinished

An invitation
To start
Where you stopped

A place holder
To complete
Those stories

A time marker
Of the tales
Gone by

An announcement
By the page, "My words
have been heard"

Gift of a Bookmark

A gesture
Of a friend
Saying I'm there

Show you where
we got last
& were lost

My Word, My Signature, My Honor

—

My Word, My Signature is how a mere scribble commits one for life, despite situational & contextual dynamics.

Yet those scratches on paper give it the weight of one's honor.

—

Signatures your's are your Sunshine
Always true, with the power behind
deliver to promise

My promise doesn't need a sign
My word, is of honor, should be fine

Strong in conviction, clarity when told
Spoken words yet, cannot forward or be sold

My word, has the power, to hold
To reach each—my signature—the replicating
mold

A banknote, without one
Bearers' cheque, with none

Mark sheets, prescriptions
worth not the paper,
whatever the sum

Signatures on a paper
Freeze a situation
for that duration

Beware of Words malafide
Promises beyond capacity,

immoral, illegal, or malicious
also those untold, do not hold

/

Free, fair & functional
In intent & as inked

Promises made to be kept
Whatever the unknowns missed
Reflected in wavy linked curves
Randomness in each imprint
consistent variations,
withstood time & situations
Steadfast in commitments,
despite

No doubts. No challenges.
Not diminished upon exchange

/

Signatures your's are your Sunshine
Always true, with the power behind
deliver to promise

Moon however, like mine
Reflects changes every time
Yet honored!

Postscript

Silence has no signatures
It announces its presence
A quiet resolve within
Signatures as character

Lovingly Layered Lies

—

***Lovingly Layered Lies** describes how falsehoods may serve the purpose of the moment but distort the interactions. And these anomalies have a tendency to stick & stay on eventually in an uncontrollable & costly chain reaction.*

—

White Lies

Benign falsehoods
Lovingly told lies

White lies, false stories for someone
For her to believe as true, just for fun

Is it okay making up some
Or being told one

Harmless we may say
It'll make her day
And it does!

You did achieve
to deceive
a goal yours to control.

That is where it ends
Or does it?

Where does the problem lie

Morality and judgment apart
Though that's a good place to start

Problems with the stories we cook
Roots run deeper than they look.

What is a lie?
A possibility, that did not happen
A probability of less than one

As spreads the lie
numbers multiply
Distortions amplify
Values gone by

Lies
Once told, not clarified,
seed mistrust, conflicts sprout
wild weeds entangle lives

Truth
No space for confusion.
No misrepresentation
No misinterpretation

Truth's values are definitive
occurrence is certain
Integrate they do, cumulative

Game of Falsehoods

Game of falsehoods,
a circular firing squad
concept itself is flawed

Many players & actors
Undefined unknown factors

Bound in bonds
fragile on trust
A hint of false alarm
triggers harm

Each on their own
Looking for safe corners
in a circle of fraud

Lie (low) if you must,
if it saves someone's life

A hazardous tool,
Be sure to know why
In time, do clarify, justify,
demystify!!

Not to forget we chose to ignore
& keep apart
Morality, judgment, values & more
Which also play their part

At the end of it all
a lie is lie
No matter what
And that's the
Truth!!

Buy your Own Bread

—-

Buy your Own Bread *is more of a commentary on those unique social settings where the breadwinner & breadmaker get isolated by cultural practices & cuisine preferences.*

—-

Indian subcontinent is unique
In many dimensions

Bread & Rice is one of those

/

Nowhere, that I know of,
is bread baked fresh as we eat

roti, chapati, phulka & more

Now that is great
For the appetite & cuisine

/

Bread daily, Thrice a day
Lucky if you have

What about the one
Who is rolling those pins

In circles after circles
Around the fire

They can never join you
At the table

Nor the conversation
Those bonding moments

Eventually
Out of the loop of their own life

/

Perhaps not geographically accurate
Somewhere at the subcontinent midpoint

between Aravallis & Bay of Bengal
The transition point is in that center

The middle zones, through the Vindhyas
Haryana, Uttar Pradesh, Bihar

Rice overlaps with wheat
Further east, it's mostly rice we eat

Opposite direction toward west
bread dominates the plate

/

It's only in this subcontinent
The middle zones across the globe

Where bread cooked fresh
In heat and alone

Served at the tables
with rice

Rice completes the meal
Complements the bread

Respite to the kitchen
Cooking fresh

/

Rice & bread are equal
What about the one facing the heat

Alone!

Buy your Own Bread
And another...

Cheers... with a Clink!

—

Cheers... with a Clink! *describes how the sound of clinking glasses completes the excitation of ALL five senses.*

—

Lustrous looks
Tingling sensation
Bittersweet taste
Unforgettable fragrance

Quiet in anticipation!

See, feel, taste, and smell!
the pour

Saw, felt, relished & smelt...
desire, yet for more

Spirits satiated all five senses,
Only when we heard

Cheers with a Clink!!

Happy Ours

—

Happy Ours *encourages us to make time for ourselves*

—

Walk in
Walk out

time starts
with you

Wouldn't stop
Without you

Time together or alone
Count as all-one

Only cheers
Raise bottoms up

Spirits flow
Until you go

At

Happy Ours
No Time Bar

Sinner or Saint

—

***Sinner or Saint** explores the absence or presence of good or bad in our definitions & perspectives.*

—

Love, hate
Desire & fear
Greed as well

Yet done no bad
With intent
Meant well as well

Absence of bad
Does it mean
Good?

few corners cut
Just to do good
Love for all on display

Fear i do
makes me give
More

Presence of good
Does it makeup
For my bad?

Blurred & intersecting
Good coexists with bad
That's life

Of a Sinner. Of a Saint

Ink—Black, Blue, Green & Red are four disconnected expansions of the color they represent. Just for fun...

Ink, Black... Nothing escapes

Potful of stories,
Await to appear as words
Escaping the ink black

Indelible memories,
Happy, sad, fact or fantasy
Indistinguishable in fluid black

A drop each, a familiar face
Special are the ones spelt out
Stories, memories decoded from color black

Bottled-up feelings
Unexpressed & shelved
Dry-up never escapes, their moments black

Remained in dark, what was left to write
Nudged it was, right over the edge
Nothing to hold; it's black

Hit the bottom, shattered,
Words' spell broken,
Untold stories spattered—in spots black.

Ink, Green... the envious green

Trees stuck on ground
Never to embrace

On borrowed wings,
love across the greens

feelings within
the color of envy, Green.

/

Bleached blank
As paper

Imprints in color
Tell another's story

Seldom theirs in Green
Ink, Green.., the envious green

Ink Blue... Royal, more than the King

Do Kings & Queens
Have only highs & no lows
A day away, off their throne

Do Kings & Queens,
Have the Monday blues
A day, another takes the throne

Do Kings & Queens
Have pawns they do trust
A day of Kingship, & yet no throne

/

Pawns of power
Quickly know
Royal, no more the King

Pawns in power
Quick to show
Loyal, more than the King

Ink Blue,,, Royal more than the King

Postscript

True Rulers

Rulebooks inked in blue

Ink, Red... last of a Rainbow

Spectral colors
Rain washed smile
Brightens skies

True to color
Stories told
From a mile

Refracted colors
Off new drops
Happy tales for each sky

Unwound colors
VIBGYOR
Unmixed from bright

Connected colors
Bands of life flavors
Spread edge to edge

Bridged colors
with no start
disappearing ends

Masked colors
Stories untold
Invisible beyond red

Ink, Red... last of a Rainbow

Postscript
Visible to all
Are tales of happy colors

What are your stories
Hidden beyond those reds

Readers' Notes

9 789363 305298

Printed by Libri Plureos GmbH in Hamburg, Germany